World Languages

Colours in Spanish

Daniel Nunn

www.raintreepublishers.co.uk
Visit our website to find out
more information about
Raintree books.

To order:
☎ Phone 0845 6044371
▤ Fax +44 (0) 1865 312263
▣ Email myorders@raintreepublishers.co.uk

Customers from outside the UK please telephone +44 1865 312262

Raintree is an imprint of Capstone Global Library Limited,
a company incorporated in England and Wales having its
registered office at 7 Pilgrim Street, London, EC4V 6LB
– Registered company number: 6695582

Edited by Daniel Nunn, Rebecca Rissman, and Sian Smith
Designed by Joanna Hinton-Malivoire
Picture research by Elizabeth Alexander
Production by Alison Parsons
Originated by Capstone Global Library Ltd
Printed and bound in China by South China Printing
Company Ltd

ISBN 978 1 406 239195
16 15 14 13 12
10 9 8 7 6 5 4 3 2 1

British Library Cataloguing in Publication Data
Nunn, Daniel.
    Colours in Spanish. -- (World languages. Colours)
    1. Spanish language--Vocabulary--Juvenile literature.
    2. Colors--Juvenile literature. 3. Spanish language--
    Textbooks for foreign speakers--English.
    I. Title II. Series
    468.2'421-dc23

Acknowledgements
We would like to thank Shutterstock for permission to reproduce
photographs: pp.4 (© Phiseksit), 5 (© Stephen Aaron Rees), 6
(© Tischenko Irina), 7 (© Tony Magdaraog), 8 (© szefei), 9 (©
Picsfive), 10 (© Eric Isselée), 11 (© Yasonya), 12 (© Nadezhda
Bolotina), 13 (© Maryna Gviazdovska), 14 (© Erik Lam), 15 (© Eric
Isselée), 16 (© Ruth Black), 17 (© blueskies9), 18 (© Alexander
Dashewsky), 19 (© Michele Perbellini), 20 (© Eric Isselée), 21 (©
Roman Rvachov).

Cover photographs reproduced with permission of Shutterstock:
dog (© Erik Lam), strawberry (© Stephen Aaron Rees), fish (©
Tischenko Irina). Back cover photograph of a cup reproduced with
permission of Shutterstock (© Maryna Gviazdovska).

We would like to thank Rebeca Otazua Bideganeta and Silvia
Vázquez-Fernández for their invaluable assistance in the
preparation of this book.

Every effort has been made to contact copyright holders of
material reproduced in this book. Any omissions will be rectified in
subsequent printings if notice is given to the publisher.

Contents

Rojo

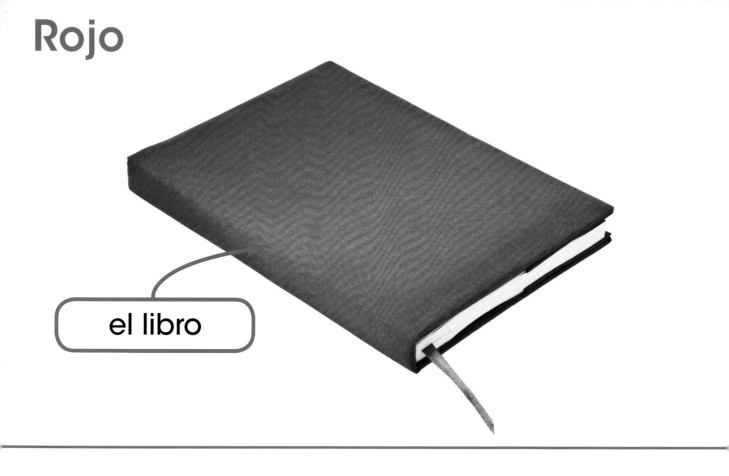

el libro

El libro es rojo.

The book is red.

la fresa

La fresa es roja.

The strawberry is red.

Naranja

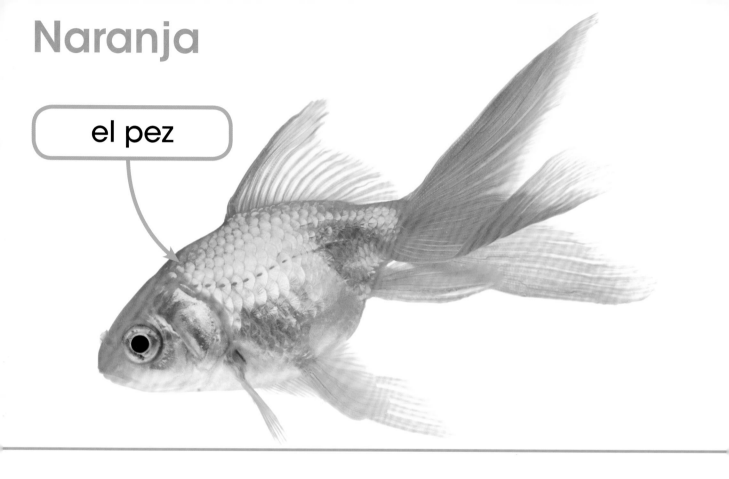

el pez

El pez es naranja.

The fish is orange.

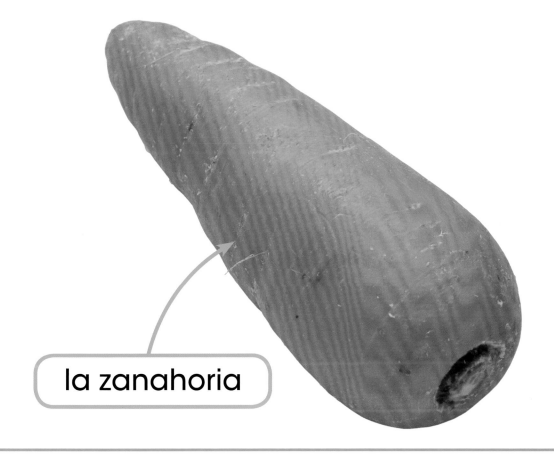

la zanahoria

La zanahoria es naranja.

The carrot is orange.

Amarillo

la flor

La flor es amarilla.

The flower is yellow.

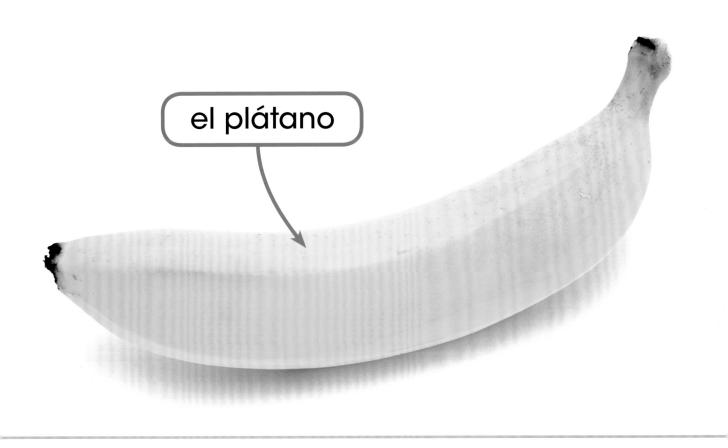

el plátano

El plátano es amarillo.

The banana is yellow.

Verde

el pájaro

El pájaro es verde.

The bird is green.

la manzana

La manzana es verde.
The apple is green.

Azul

la camiseta

La camiseta es azul.

The T-shirt is blue.

la taza

La taza es azul.

The cup is blue.

Marrón

el perro

El perro es marrón.

The dog is brown.

la vaca

La vaca es marrón.

The cow is brown.

Rosa

la torta

La torta es rosa.

The cake is pink.

el sombrero

El sombrero es rosa.

The hat is pink.

Blanca

la leche

La leche es blanca.

The milk is white.

la nieve

La nieve es blanca.

The snow is white.

Negro

El gato es **negro**.

The cat is **black**.

el paraguas

El paraguas es **negro**.
The umbrella is **black**.

Dictionary

Spanish word	How to say it	English word
amarilla	a-ma-ree-ya	yellow (feminine)
amarillo	a-ma-ree-yo	yellow (masculine)
azul	a-thul	blue
blanca	blan-ca	white
camiseta	cam-ee-say-ta	T-shirt
el	el	the (masculine)
es	es	is
flor	floor	flower
fresa	fray-sa	strawberry
gato	gat-o	cat
la	la	the (feminine)
leche	letch-ay	milk
libro	lee-bro	book
manzana	man-than-na	apple
marrón	mar-ron	brown
naranja	na-ran-ha	orange

Spanish word	How to say it	English word
negro	neh-gro	black
nieve	nee-eh-beh	snow
pájaro	paa-ha-ro	bird
paraguas	pah-raa-gwas	umbrella
perro	per-ro	dog
pez	peth	fish
plátano	plaa-tan-o	banana
roja	ro-ha	red (feminine)
rojo	ro-ho	red (masculine)
rosa	ro-sa	pink
sombrero	som-brer-o	hat
taza	ta-tha	cup
torta	tort-ta	cake
vaca	bac-a	cow
verde	bear-day	green
zanahoria	than-a-horia	carrot

See words in the "How to say it" columns for a rough guide to pronunciations.

Index

Notes for parents and teachers

In Spanish, nouns are either masculine or feminine. The word for "the" changes accordingly – either el (masculine) or la (feminine). Sometimes adjectives have different spellings too, depending on whether the noun is masculine or feminine. This is why some of the colours have more than one spelling.